IN FULL BLOOM

COLORING BOOK

RUTH SOFFER

DOVER PUBLICATIONS, INC.
MINEOLA, NEW YORK

Note

There is nothing more beautiful than seeing—and smelling—a flower in full bloom! In this coloring book we have selected an assortment of blossoms ranging from the most dramatic blossom like the eight- to ten-inch amaryllis flower to the small, delicate petals of the chrysanthemum. Each flower has been identified for easy reference. Use pencils, crayons, or markers to color the pages any way you like.

Bibliographical Note

In Full Bloom Coloring Book, published by Dover Publications, Inc., in 2014, is a republication of plates from *In Full Bloom: A Close-Up Coloring Book,* originally published by Dover in 2012.

International Standard Book Number

ISBN-13: 978-0-486-49453-1
ISBN-10: 0-486-49453-5

Manufactured in the United States by RR Donnelley
49453507   2015
www.doverpublications.com

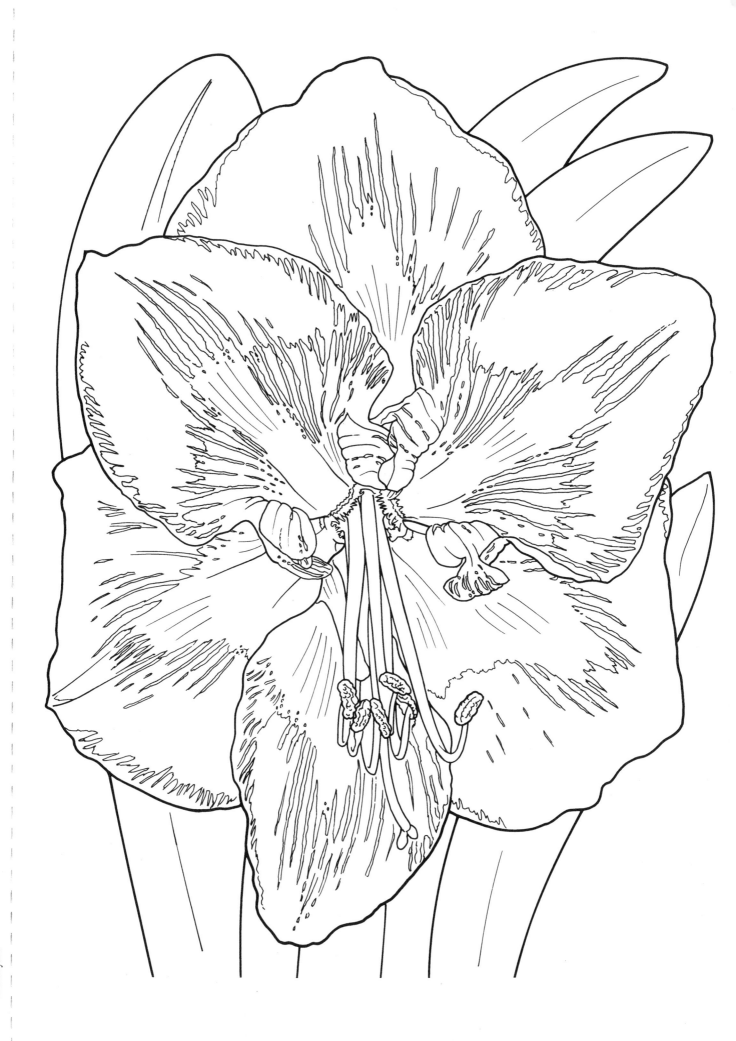

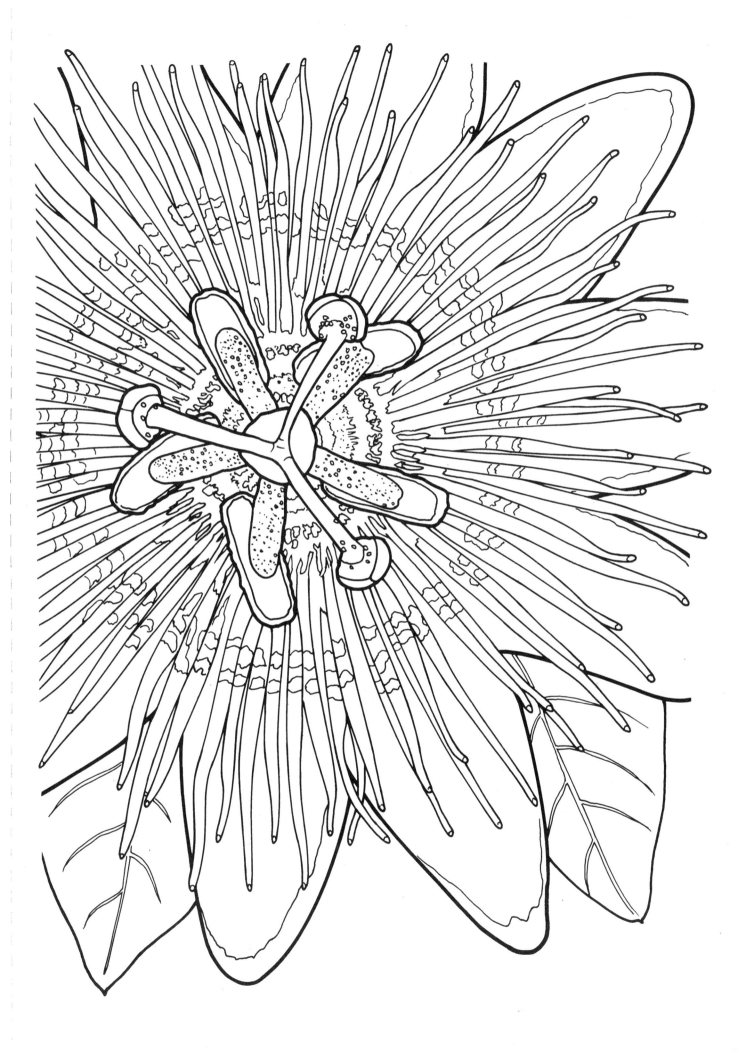

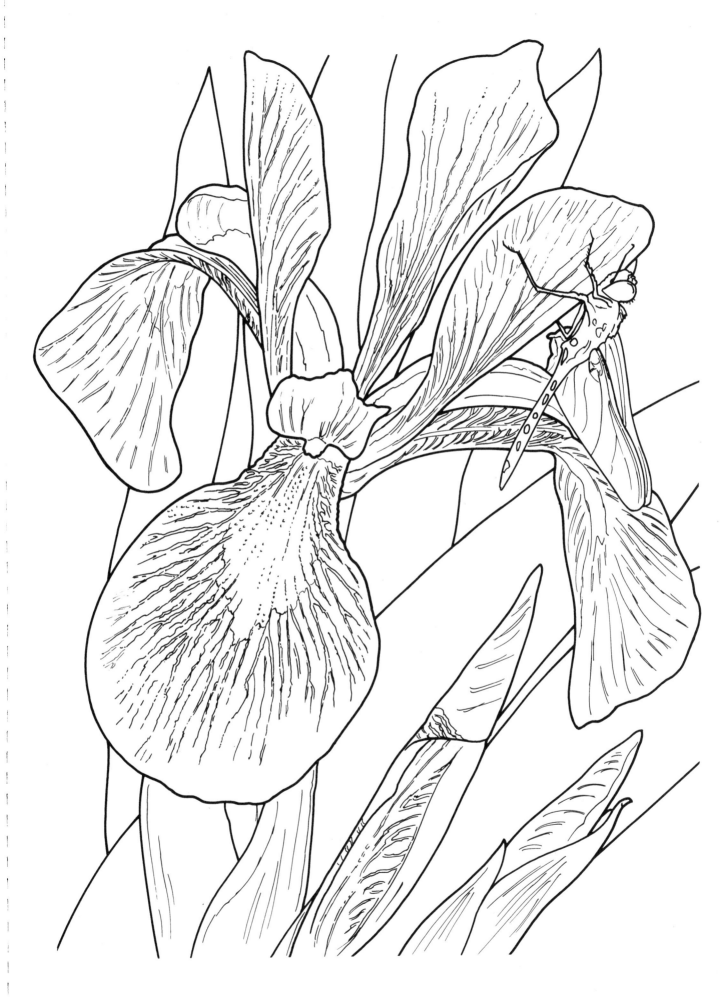